SIGNING
FOR
READING
SUCCESS

Jan C. Hafer
Robert M. Wilson

CLERC BOOKS
Gallaudet University Press
Washington, D.C.

Kendall Green Publications
An imprint of Gallaudet University Press
Washington, DC 20002

Published 1986
12 11 10 09 08 07 06 05 13 12 11 10 09 08 07 06
Printed in the United States of America

ISBN 0-930323-18-1

Signs in this booklet are from *The Signed English Starter* and *The Comprehensive Signed English Dictionary* and are used by permission of Gallaudet University, Washington, D.C.

CONTENTS

ACKNOWLEDGMENTS

This booklet represents several years of research and work done by many other teachers. While we cannot name every teacher who participated in this research and work, there are several who need to be specifically recognized.

Mrs. Karen Arick, a reading teacher in St. Mary's County, Maryland, and her principal, Dr. Patricia Russavage, opened their school to our ideas and collected important data on the effects of signing with beginning readers who were struggling with the retention of sight vocabulary.

Mrs. Judy Hoyer, the project director for the Primary Project in Prince George's County, Maryland, and her staff opened doors and provided important data for the notion that signing and fingerspelling could help early readers and writers who were not meeting with success with traditional instruction.

Mrs. Marianne Teague, a first grade teacher in Prince George's County, Maryland, shared with us her efforts to help first graders use signing and fingerspelling to improve their spelling skills.

The teachers in Berkeley County, West Virginia, helped us with Jan Hafer's research. They managed to keep us classroom oriented. Their long-term commitment to the use of signing and fingerspelling has been very encouraging.

We also acknowledge the Gallaudet University Press staff for their granting us the opportunity to share our work with classroom teachers by publishing this booklet. Their enthusiasm for this project and their editorial assistance have been greatly appreciated.

As you read and decide to become involved with this instructional strategy, we invite you to communicate with us about your results. Your sharing can only result in providing further assistance to others in helping children become better readers and spellers.

ABOUT THE AUTHORS

Jan C. Hafer is a teacher in the Family Education and Early Intervention Department at the Maryland School for the Deaf in Frederick. She received her doctorate in education from the University of Maryland in 1984. She has conducted research and workshops on the use of signing with hearing children for the past several years.

Robert M. Wilson is Professor of Education and Director of the Reading Center at the University of Maryland in College Park. He is currently interest in research on the use of signs with hearing students as a reinforcement for sight word learning. Dr. Wilson is also working as a consultant to the National Captioning Institute for their research efforts on the effects of closed captioned television as a medium for reading instruction with hearing and hearing-impaired students.

INTRODUCTION

While signs were developed to help hearing-impaired people communicate with each other and with those who hear, other uses for signing have evolved. Special educators have used signing frequently to assist learning-disabled, aphasic, and autistic populations as a supplementary means of communication.

A lesser known application of signing is its use with non-handicapped hearing children. This booklet was prepared for teachers of hearing children to help them use signing in reading and language arts instruction. The concept is simple: When introducing new words to children, sign the words while pronouncing them and have the children do the same.

Why sign words to hearing children? Since the 1800s, some educators of deaf students have recommended the use of signing to develop reading, spelling, and written language skills with children who can hear. These educators observed that the hearing siblings of their deaf students profited from learning signs and recommended the use of signing to the teachers of hearing children. Current interest in the use of signing for hearing populations has received considerable attention. Reports of its potential as an instructional strategy are appearing in various journals and books.

The reluctance of many teachers to use the signing strategy with hearing children is based on several myths.

1. I can't learn signs.
2. It takes too much time to learn signs.
3. Signs might become a crutch for the children.
4. I don't know how to use signs for reading and language arts.

This booklet was designed to dispel these myths and to help teachers understand the simplicity and effectiveness of signs. It is based on Signed English developed at Gallaudet University, Washington, D.C. Signed English "is a manual English system designed to be used with speech. It is a semantic system in which the signs...represent the meanings of words found in standard English dictionaries. They do not represent the spelling or the sound of those words... Signed English is by far the simplest manual English system in general use..." It " serves two basic purposes. First, it is a model of the English language. Second, it is used to communicate information between people (Bornstein & Saulnier, 1984, pp. viii-ix). Teachers who want to learn more about Signed English should read the introductory material in *The Comprehensive Signed English Dictionary* and *The Signed English Starter,* the basic references for this booklet.

It is true that many teachers do not know how to sign. The ideal situation, of course, would be for teachers wanting to incorporate signing in their classes of hearing children to take a class in sign language. This is not always possible and, in this situation, not necessary. None of the teachers in the studies on which this booklet is based had taken a sign language class. A teacher who studies the two references mentioned earlier can learn to sign the words necessary to carry out the following activities. Not only do the books include a drawing of each sign, but a description is also given. By looking at the pictures and reading the descriptions, a teacher can learn to sign well enough to incorporate it into the classroom routine.

MAJOR TEACHING CONCEPTS AND SIGNING

Three words in the professional literature that every teacher knows are *imagery,* *multisensory,* and *motivation.* How does signing incorporate these three concepts into classroom instruction?

Imagery

The use of imagery is an effective technique for teaching the meaning of particular words. The idea is for the children to form a mental picture of the concept of the printed word they are learning. Signing is a particularly effective strategy to use because of the picturelike quality of many signs. When students sign words, they are visually and motorically "echoing" the concept. Look at the following illustrations of three signs. As you sign each one, think of the characteristics of the word that you see or feel in the sign itself.

house
Place tips of both hands together to form roof. Move apart and down to form sides of house.

drink
Mime holding drinking glass of water with C shape RH.

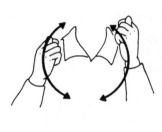

truck
Mime holding and moving steering wheel with T shape hands, palms facing.

As you sign the words you can see and feel the meaning inherent in each one. For this reason many signs are said to be iconic; that is, these signs indicate meaning by the way they are made.

Multisensory

With many students who have difficulty learning and also with those who are very young, a multisensory approach can be very effective. By tapping kinesthetic-tactile avenues as well as the visual and auditory avenues, the child is utilizing many means of learning. It is often difficult for the teacher to plan learning activities in which children can be physically involved. Signing provides a way that teachers can help students to use many of their senses in learning. It has been observed that when students are physically involved through signing, they are also attending to the task.

Motivation

It is a fact that motivation plays an important role in learning. Teachers are constantly seeking ways to motivate children to become involved in the learning process. Teachers and students alike have noted the motivational aspects of signing. Teachers say signing is motivating for them because it is effective and offers instructional variety. Students say that signing is fun and that they can show their parents and friends a new form of communication.

POPULATIONS WHO CAN BENEFIT FROM SIGNING

In the best of worlds everyone would learn to sign for the purpose of communicating with the 14 million hearing-impaired people in the United States today. The interest and need are there, but in most schools the curriculum does not include instruction in signing.

For the purpose of this booklet signing is viewed as an excellent reinforcer for the retention of sight vocabulary and for accuracy in spelling. Several populations appear to be in need of this type of reinforcement.

Many students in kindergarten and first grade have retention problems. But these students have not yet met with the frustration of repeated failures in learning to read. The inclusion of signing in initial instruction can make early reading experiences successful for many of them.

Beginning Reading Students

In St. Mary's County, Maryland, four first-grade pupils were identified by their teacher as being unable to function in their basal readers. This teacher and the school's reading teacher started instruction with the use of signing. The four children began to retain their sight vocabulary, learned an average of 80 words in 8 weeks, and started reading in their basal readers. Had signing not been initiated, these four first graders probably would have ended up in remedial reading classes later.

Most teachers know students who have difficulty retaining sight vocabulary. The visual/auditory methods used to teach sight vocabulary are simply insufficient to help many students. These students are found in remedial reading, adult literacy, and special education classes. Too often the teaching strategies in these classes are to offer more of what did not work during regular instruction—more phonics, more sight drills, more oral reading—and the result is more frustration. Most of these students will find signing beneficial. Once they find success with a signing reinforcement technique, attitudes change and the world of reading becomes open to them.

Remedial Reading Students

Classrooms in this country are experiencing an influx of students who speak little or no English. These ESOL (English as a Second Language) students are finding schooling to be a frustrating process. They are eager to learn English and to be able to read in English. At times there are no ESOL resource services available, and classroom teachers are expected to provide meaningful instruction—an extremely frustrating teaching assignment for most teachers. The iconicity of many signs makes signing a logical choice for initial instruction of these students.

ESOL Students

A seven-year-old boy from Nigeria had little English and was becoming a behavior problem in his classroom. With private tutoring he responded immediately to signing and was able to learn to pronounce and read many English words. His perceptive classroom teacher had him share the signs that he learned with his classmates; he knew something that they did not know! As he experienced success in school his behavior problems diminished.

3

Hearing-Impaired Students

Students with hearing impairment are being mainstreamed in public school classrooms all across America. The inclusion of signing in regular classroom instruction could benefit these hearing-impaired students by (1) providing visual cues when the auditory (spoken) cues are unclear, and (2) encouraging hearing students to develop their signing skills to communicate more easily with their hearing-impaired friends.

Learning-Disabled Students

Students with learning disabilities are also being mainstreamed into regular classrooms for most of the day. They usually have been diagnosed as having processing problems that cause them trouble with reading and spelling. For many, instruction via signing can help them overcome the processing problems and provide them with successful experiences in reading and spelling.

Spelling Students

Some students seem to be able to read without difficulty but have a terrible time with spelling. Teachers have found that many students benefit from having their spelling words taught through fingerspelling. Reinforcing spelling skills with fingerspelling adds a multisensory element to the phonetic decoding of words.

SIGNING STRATEGIES

In this section strategies for using signs for instruction with hearing children are presented. Strategies for sight vocabulary, phonics, and language arts instruction as well as for classroom management are included.

Many students have difficulty remembering sight vocabulary. They may have been asked to focus on word configuration (e.g., look), to sound out familiar parts (e.g., *pen*cil), or to sound out letters (e.g., c-a-t). These strategies are based on sound instructional practice and work with many children. When these strategies fail, however, most teachers have nothing to try but to repeat instruction with those same strategies that have not worked. Often the children continue to have difficulty with retention of sight vocabulary.

The introduction of signs to reinforce sight vocabulary is an easy strategy for teachers to try. The steps are as follows.

1. Determine the sight words to be taught and locate the signs in *The Comprehensive Signed English Dictionary* or *The Signed English Starter*. For example, if the words to be taught in a given lesson are *tree, house, truck, drive,* and *look,* then the sign for each word is needed.

tree
Five shape RH palm left. Place right elbow on back of LH and shake RH rapidly.

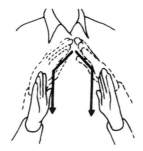

house
Place tips of both hands together to form roof. Move apart and down to form sides of house.

truck
Mime holding and moving steering wheel with T shape hands, palms facing.

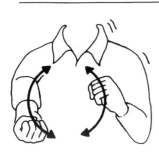

drive
A shape both hands. Move as if turning steering wheel of a car. (Sometimes made with two D shapes.)

look
Point to eyes with tips of right V, then twist and point out.

2. Introduce each word to the children. Show them the word. Then show them the sign and pronounce the word.
3. Involve the children. Show them the word again. Have them make the sign and pronounce the word.
4. Repeat this process several times for each word.

It is often essential for the teacher to discuss the iconic nature of a sign. For example, the sign for *house* outlines a basic house configuration. The sign for *truck* is the sign for *drive* made with the manual alphabet *t*, using both hands. Children might not grasp the iconicity of a given sign, however, without some explanation. Once they understand that signs convey meanings, when they see a word, they think of the meaning of the word, sign it, and then pronounce it.

If the words are repeatedly reinforced using the signing strategy, most children will learn the words easily and retain them as their sight vocabulary. It has been observed that once a word is well locked in the child's memory, the use of the sign for that word will be discontinued independently by the child.

The use of signs to reinforce sight vocabulary is really that simple. As stated before, children enjoy learning with this strategy and find themselves being quite successful. See the research section (pp. 12-15) for data that show just how successful it can be.

Phonics

Many children have difficulty with the phonics approach to reading. Teachers may not be at liberty to use an alternative approach; however, they can follow the regular teaching procedure for any lesson in phonics but enhance the lesson with signing to provide students with multisensory input as well as an emphasis on imagery.

There are two techniques teachers can use when incorporating signing into a phonics lesson. One is to *sign* the word to emphasize its meaning. The other is to *fingerspell* the word to emphasize the sound and "feel" of the letters. When there is a similarity between the printed and manual symbol, it should be pointed out to the students. If the students are learning the sound, then they could respond with the manual letter for that sound as they say it in a word.

Language Arts

Many signs found in *The Comprehensive Signed English Dictionary* and *The Signed English Starter* are iconic. This iconic element is helpful in demonstrating the meanings of the words being taught. The following signs may be used for primary-level lessons on opposites.

up
Point index finger up.

down
Point index finger down.

6

open
B shape both hands, palms down, tips out, index fingers touching. Arc apart, ending with palms up.

close (verb)
B shape both hands, palms facing, tips out. Turn toward each other so that index fingers touch.

come
One shape hands, knuckles up, tips out. Bring tips up and back toward chest.

go
One shape both hands, palms and index tips in. Flip index tips out, ending with palms up.

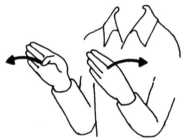

big
B shape both hands, palms facing, tips out. Move away from one another.

little
L shape both hands, palms facing, index tips out. Move close together.

in
C shape LH palm right. Place tips of right flat O into left C.

out
Cupped 5 shape LH palm right. Place fingers of RH against left palm and pull out, ending in flat O shape.

When teaching the signs for opposites, the teacher may present one sign and say, "Can you show me the opposite with your hands?" The students will be able to sign the appropriate sign without formal instruction. The teacher should again emphasize the picturelike quality of each sign.

Drama

Signing gives communication a whole new dimension. Its richness and beauty make sign language a natural avenue of artistic expression. Adding signing to oral reading can help the student focus on the meaning of the passage and the correct dramatic interpretation. Students can learn how to express themselves with their bodies. Ask students to interpret a word or concept with mime and then compare it to the sign for that word. How are the mime and sign similar? How are they different?

Signing can enhance the beauty of lyrics and rhythm in song. When the annual music program rolls around, the addition of a few songs in sign adds a sparkle to the show. Sheet music is available that includes signs for important words in the songs (see *Songs in Signed English* and *You've Got a Song*, p. 16).

Classroom Management

"Sit down," "Line up," "Quiet, please." These and similar routine classroom management phrases can become almost meaningless after they are repeated day after day. Signing them to the students offers a change of pace and assures attention. One can suddenly stop talking, flick the lights, and silently sign, "Sit down, please," or "Line up, please." The children will do as they are told.

sit
H shape both hands, palm down, left tips slanted right, right tips slanted left. Rest right H on left.

down
Point index finger down.

please
Rub right palm in clockwise circle against upper chest.

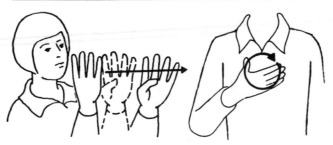

line up
Four shape both hands, left palm right, right palm left. Place right hand behind left then move LH forward.

please
Rub right palm in clockwise circle against upper chest.

8

One teacher instructed his students to silently sign to him questions such as "Rest room, please?" and "Water, please?" at times when a quiet classsroom was desirable—when he was teaching or during a work period. The teacher responded with the sign for yes or no.

rest room
R shape RH palm down.
Bounce to right.

please
Rub right palm in clockwise circle against upper chest.

water
Tap lips (or chin) twice with index finger of right W.

please
Rub right palm in clockwise circle against upper chest.

yes
S shape RH. Shake up and down at wrist.

no
Snap middle finger, index and thumb together quickly.

With reduced distractions, the students remained on task and understood the signs from the teacher.

At times when there are a few minutes to spare, keeping eyes and hands busy with signing will keep hands out of trouble. The teacher can silently fingerspell names for lining up. All the students pay attention because they don't want to miss their names.

FINGERSPELLING STRATEGIES

Fingerspelling is using the manual alphabet to spell words. Each letter is represented by a handshape. Fingerspelling can be used to teach spelling skills and phonics skills to the students. When fingerspelling, it is best to say the word, not the individual letters, as it is fingerspelled. This presents the word as a whole unit. Try fingerspelling the following words as you say them.

cat   house   black

The following characteristics of signing also apply to fingerspelling.

Iconicity   Look at the following letters:

o v w y c i j l z

Do you see a similarity between the manual symbol and the printed symbol? Some manual symbols are less similar to their printed counterparts, but a similarity does exit. The following letters are examples:

d e t u m n a

Multisensory   As children fingerspell words, they are physically experiencing each letter. Their attention is focused on the function of the letters within a word. Experienced fingerspellers have reported that when encountering a new word to be learned, they will fingerspell it to lock it in their memory.

Motivation   Children are excited to learn to spell with their fingers. They can practice words silently with each other. They can spell messages across the room. They like the change from a strictly paper and pencil task.

Following are some ideas for using fingerspelling:
1. Introduce new spelling words through fingerspelling.
2. Conduct silent spelling bees using fingerspelling.
3. Pair children to silently review spelling words during free time using fingerspelling.
4. When spelling words with similar patterns, emphasize that the words "feel" almost the same when fingerspelling them (e.g., *cat, rat, hat, mat*).

The American Manual Alphabet

A B C D E F G

H I J K L M

N O P Q R S

T U V W X Y Z

RESEARCH

The use of sign language in the deaf community has had a rich yet controversial history. While it is the basic form of communication among many deaf people, some people view it as an undesirable crutch. It is expected to have a similar reaction among hearing educators as the idea of signing to assist with reading instruction gains attention. An attempt has been made, therefore, to develop empirical support for its use with hearing children who are experiencing difficulty with the learning-to-read process. Signing for reading is multisensory, it is a code, and it is motivating to young children. It is not believed to be a crutch, but rather a reinforcement to regualr instruction in reading. Children apparently stop using signas as soon as they have mastered the sight words or the spelling of words, but more needs to be known. What are the effects of sign reinforcement with hearing children?

Four Studies

The following four studies provide some answers. It would seem that signing and fingerspelling are acceptable alternatives to regular instruction when a reader is floundering with regular instructional techniques. They are obviously not a cure-all for every floundering child—for some the answers are elsewhere. But, these data do hold promise for many. The studies are presented so that much of the emotional arguments can be laid to rest and teachers can rely upon some data which were carefully collected and analyzed.

Number 1

A reading teacher worked with 11 first-grade students to help reinforce their sight vocabulary with signs (Arick, 1984). She compared their retention of sight words during traditional instruction with their retention during sign instruction. Sight-word retention during regular instruction was 58% and during sign instruction 79%. These children were selected for sign instruction because they were making slow progress during regular instruction. Two of the 11 children did not profit from sign instruction. Four were making slow progress in regular instruction but retained 100% of the words introduced during sign instruction.

Number 2

Hoyer (Wilson & Hoyer, 1985) collected data on 10 first-grade children over a period of 14 weeks. She also compared regular instruction with sign instruction. Children were selected for study because of their difficulty in retaining sight vocabulary. During regular instruction they averaged a retention of 69% of their sight words over the 14 weeks. During sign instruction they averaged 93% retention. The use of sign for instruction with early readers has now been included in the "Primary Project Teacher's Guide" in Prince George's County, Maryland.

Number 3

Teague (Wilson, Teague, & Teague, 1985) used fingerspelling and signs to help first-grade children with their spelling. She selected seven first-graders who were spelling between 25% and 46% of their words accurately. When using fingerspelling and signs, they improved to between 56% and 90% spelling accuracy. Teague also checked retention of spelling words at the end of the study and found the fingerspelling and sign instructional words were retained between 60% and 90% in accuracy.

As previously mentioned none of the teachers in these studies had taken course work in signing. They all relied upon the use of *The Comprehensive Signed English Dictionary* (Bornstein, Saulnier, & Hamilton, 1983). The teachers were instructed to select the words for study and check the dictionary for the appropriate signs. Then they introduced the words, demonstrated the signs, and had the children make the signs while saying the words.

Teachers in Berkeley County, West Virginia, have made use of signing for reading instruction for the past 10 years. Recently, an experiment was conducted to determine if research findings would support the teachers' enthusiasm for the technique (Hafer, 1984). A single subject research design using 10 students was employed.

The primary age, learning-disabled students were first taught sight words with a tracing technique and then with signing. Initially the tracing technique was employed. The students were taught four sets of six words each. After each set the students were tested for retention.

The primary age, learning-disabled students were taught sight words with tracing and signing. Again, the students were tested after each set of words was taught.

Following the signing, a return to tracing was employed for two sets of six words each. The test scores were recorded for each student. One case is presented in Figure 1. (Hafer, 1984, p. 37).

Number of Correct Words			
6		x—x—x	
5		x	
4			
3	x—x		x—x
2	x x		
1			
0			
Week	1 2 3 4 A*	5 6 7 8 B*	9 10 A*

Figure 1. Single Case Data for One Subject.

Figure 1 indicates that the student learned about one-half of the words using tracing and all or nearly all when using signing. Of the 10 students participating, 7 had patterns similar to Figure 1.

In addition to the sight-word accuracy records, data were collected about teacher and student responses to the two methods used. All students responded with a preference for the signing technique. All teachers also preferred using the signing technique and indicated that they planned to continue to use it.

As teachers begin to use signs and fingerspelling they might want to conduct their own research. This research can provide support when accountability questions are raised.

Single Subject Research

The use of Single Subject Research is recommended (Kazdin, 1982). One student is studied at a time. The student serves as his or her own control, and data are collected to compare regular instruction with either sign or fingerspelling instruction. This research design is ideal for classroom teachers. Here are the steps to follow. Use the Data Collection Sheet to record the information. Feel free to duplicate the form on page 18. On the Data Collection Sheet, under method, please indicate what was used for instruction in Baseline.

Step 1. Select a student who is experiencing considerable difficulty retaining sight vocabulary. Describe that student's behavior as carefully as possible.

Step 2. Collect student performance in regular instruction for a 4-week period. Test for sight-word retention at the end of each week. These data are "Baseline" information, Labeled A on the form.

Step 3. Change instruction to use signs for 6 to 8 weeks. Collect the same data as in Step 2. These new data are "Intervention" information, labeled B.

Step 4. Return to regular instruction for 3 weeks. Collect the same data as in Step 2. This new step is "Return to Baseline," labeled A^2.

Step 5. Return to sign for 3 weeks. Collect the data the same way. This is "Return to Intervention," labeled B^2.

Step 6. This step is optional. A sample of words from A and A^2 and a sample from B and B^2 can be selected to determine the long-term effect of both types of instruction.

Figure 2 in an example of how data might look when placed on a Single Subject Figure. The data are analyzed for educational significance. The student's performance in A (Baseline) was one of low achievement and of a stable pattern; that is, the performance did not vary much. During B (Intervention), achievement improved and was accelerating; that is, achievement was moving toward desired learning. A^2 showed a return to low achievement and was stable. B^2 showed a return to improved achievement and was accelerating. A, over time, showed poor retention while B, over time, showed good retention.

Following are some advantages of Single Subject Research:

1. Data are collected from many points in time. Therefore, a single good or a single poor performance will not lead to making an inaccurate conclusion.
2. Data used are the natural performances of the child. There is no need to rely upon formal testing.
3. Data can easily be evaluated visually. A glance at the figure can supply an answer to the question, "Is this technique working for this child?"

The major limitation of Single Subject Research is one of generalizability. In all of the studies previously mentioned the design was replicated on more than one child. If performance is consistent in replications, then the limitation of generalizability can be overcome.

Percentage of Words Learned	N Words Attempted															
	6	5	4	5	5	5	5	5	5	5	5	5	5	5	30	40
100					x—x—x			x—x					x—x			
95																x
90																
85																
80							x									
75																
70																
65																
60										x—x						
55																
50	x		x												x	
45																
40		x		x												
35																
30																
25																
20																
15																
10																
5																
0																
Week	1	2	3	4	5	6	7	8	9	10	11	12	13	14	15A*	15B*
			A*				B**				A*		B**			

A* Baseline — traditional
B** Intervention — Signing

Figure 2. Example of ABAB Data.

The authors would be delighted to hear the results of any Single Subject Research using signing or fingerspelling with hearing students. Students' names, the teacher's name, or the school's name will not be used in any way without written permission. Please send data to Dr. Jan C. Hafer, Maryland School for the Deaf, Frederick, MD 21701 or Dr. Robert M. Wilson, The Reading Center, University of Maryland, College Park, MD 20742.

ANNOTATED BIBLIOGRAPHY

Arick, K. (1984). [The use of signs with first graders]. Unpublished raw data.
Data collected on carefully conducted research but not written up or published.

Bornstein, H., & Saulnier, K. (1984). *The signed English starter.* Washington,
DC: Kendall Green Publications, Gallaudet University Press.
An excellent, inexpensive beginning reference for learning sign vocabulary.
The text consists of 940 basic signs taken from *The Comprehensive Signed
English Dictionary* and presented topically.

Bornstein, H., & Saulnier, K., & Hamilton, L. (1983). *The comprehensive
signed English dictionary.* Washington, DC: Kendall Green Publications,
Gallaudet University Press.
An expanded version of the original *The Signed English Dictionary.* Includes
over 3,000 illustrated signs, fingerspelling illustrations, signs for numbers, and
much more. Signs are presented alphabetically making it easy to locate a
given sign.

Bornstein, H., & Saulnier, K., & Hamilton, L. (1984). *Songs in signed English.*
Washington, DC: Kendall Green Publications, Gallaudet University
Press.
Contains eight well-known nursery songs. This Signed English children's
book, which includes music, words, and signs for each song, comes with a 33
1/3 rpm recording of the songs.

Gadling, D., & Pokorny, D. (1979). *You've got a song.* Silver Spring, MD: National Association of the Deaf.
Presents the music and signs for eight popular songs and some tips for helping students use them.

Greenberg, J., Vernon, M., DuBois, J., & McKnight, J. (1982). *The language
arts handbook.* Baltimore, MD: University Park Press.
Presents suggestions for language arts lessons that involve fingerspelling and
signing. Includes a bibliography of the major works that have been published
on this topic.

Hafer, J. C. (1984). *The effects of signing as a multisensory technique for
teaching sight vocabulary to learning disabled students.* Unpublished
doctoral dissertation. University of Maryland.
Presents data from 10 single subject research studies. Student and
teacher perceptions comparing signing and tracing are included.

Kazdin, A. (1982). *Single-case research design.* New York: Oxford University
Press.
A complete text on single subject research. Discusses assumptions, strengths,
and weaknesses of this research technique. Provides details of rules and
procedures.

Wilson, R., & Hoyer, J. (1985). The use of signing as a reinforcement of sight vocabulary in the primary grades. *1985 Yearbook of the State of Maryland International Reading Association,* pp. 43-51.
Presents data from 10 single subject research studies. Teachers used signs to reinforce sight vocabulary in grades one and two.

Wilson, R., Teague, J., & Teague, M. (1985). The use of signing and fingerspelling to improve spelling performance with hearing children. *Reading Psychology, 4,* 267-273.
Presents data from seven single subject research studies. This teacher used signs and fingerspelling to reinforce spelling with first-graders.

Classroom Materials

Manual Alphabet Poster, Gallaudet University Press .
A large (23″ x 36″), brightly colored poster of the ABCs with their corresponding manual letters.

Children's Sign Language Playing Cards, National Association of the Deaf.
Playing cards for games such as Concentration, Fish, and Old Maid. The deck consists of pairs of pictures and their corresponding signs. Children love these and learn signs quickly on their own.

Data Collection Sheet

School _____ Teacher _____

Type of Intervention _____ Reading Teacher _____

	Week	No. of Words Attempted	No. of Words Learned
A	1	_____	_____
	2	_____	_____
	3	_____	_____
	4	_____	_____
B	5	_____	_____
	6	_____	_____
	7	_____	_____
	8	_____	_____
	9	_____	_____
	10	_____	_____
A^2	11	_____	_____
	12	_____	_____
	13	_____	_____
B^2	14	_____	_____
	15	_____	_____
	16	_____	_____

		Words retained over time
	17	
A	O/T	A sample of ten words from 1, 2, 3, 4, 11, 12, 13 _____
B	O/T	A sample of ten words from 5, 6, 7, 8, 9, 10, 14, 15, 16 _____

Student description

Age _____

Grade _____

Reading level _____

Race _____

Nationality _____

Teacher perception of student attitude

	Good	Fair	Poor
Toward A	_____	_____	_____
Toward B	_____	_____	_____

Method

Describe treatment in Baseline:

Source of sight words:

Comments

ISBN 0-930323-18-1

90000>

9 780930 323189

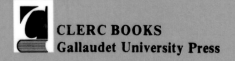

CLERC BOOKS
Gallaudet University Press